Policy Development for Special Educational Needs: A Primary School Approach

by

KATHLEEN LUTON

NASEN

A NASEN Publication

Published in 1995

© Kathleen Luton

All rights reserved.
Appendix C (pages 32 to 33), Appendix D (pages 34 to 35) and Appendix E (pages 36 to 39) are copyright but may be photocopied for reasonable use within the school which purchases this book. No other part of this publication may be reproduced or transmitted in any form or by any means, electronic, mechanical, photocopying, recording, or otherwise without the prior permission of the publishers.

ISBN 0 906730 75 9

The right of the Author to be identified as author of this work has been asserted by her in accordance with the Copyright, Designs and Patents Act 1988.

NASEN

Published by NASEN Enterprises Ltd.
NASEN Enterprises is a company limited by guarantee, registered in England and Wales. Company No. 2637438.

Further copies of this book and details of NASEN's many other publications may be obtained from the Publications Department at its registered office:
NASEN HOUSE, 4/5 Amber Business Village, Amber Close, Amington, Tamworth B77 4RP
(Tel: 01827 311500; Fax: 01827 313005)

Cover design by Graphic Images.
Typeset in Times and printed in the United Kingdom by Impress Printers (Stoke-on-Trent) Ltd.

Policy Development for Special Educational Needs: A Primary School Approach

Contents

		Page
1.	Introduction	5
2.	Reasons for Formulating a Policy	6
3.	A Whole School Approach to Policy Development	6
4.	The Timescale	10
5.	The Contents of Policy	10
	5.1 Summary Statement	10
	5.2 Objectives	11
	5.3 The Management of Special Educational Needs	12
	5.4 Admission Arrangements	13
	5.5 SEN Specialisms and Special Units	14
	5.6 Access for Disabled Pupils and Adults	15
	5.7 The Allocation of Resources	15
	5.8 Identification and Assessment; Record Keeping and Review	16
	5.9 Integration Arrangements	17
	5.10 Parental Involvement	18
	5.11 LEA Support Services	19
	5.12 Links with Health, Social Services and Voluntary Organisations	19
	5.13 Links with Other Mainstream and Special Schools	19
	5.14 Experience, Qualifications and In-service Training	19
	5.15 Success Criteria for School Policies	20
	5.16 Dealing with Parents' Complaints	22
6.	Additional Guidelines	22
	6.1 Classroom Support	23
	6.2 Planning for Individual Needs	23
	6.3 Differentiation	23
	6.4 Paired/Shared Reading	24
7.	The Monitoring and Reporting Arrangements	24
8.	Producing a Policy for Special Educational Needs	25
9.	Appendix A - Classroom Support	26
	Appendix B - Planning	27
	Appendix C - Differentiation	32
	Appendix D - Shared Reading	34
	Appendix E - The Special Needs Policy Review Guide	36
	Appendix F - Action Plan for Special Needs Policy Development	40
10.	References and Further Reading	41

Acknowledgements

The author and publishers wish to express their grateful thanks to:

- HMSO for permission to quote from Paragraphs 2.11 and 2.14 (pages 9 and 10) and Paragraph 2.33 (page 14) of *Code of Practice on the Identification and Assessment of Special Educational Needs* (1994) which is Crown Copyright. Crown Copyright is reproduced with permission of the Controller of HMSO;

- The Pupil and School Support Services and SEN Co-ordinators (SENCos) in Birmingham who have helped in devising the Individual Education Plans (IEPs) which are reproduced as examples in Appendix B.

- Archbishop Ilsley School, Birmingham, which provided ideas for Appendix D.

The author wishes to make it clear that the views expressed in this publication are her own views and not necessarily those of the Birmingham LEA.

Introduction

This booklet sets out guidance about writing and updating special needs policies. The main reference documents for carrying out this task are:-

- *The Code of Practice on the Identification and Assessment of Special Educational Needs, 1994;*

- *Circular 6.94 on the Organisation of Special Educational Provision,* published alongside the *Code;*

- *Education (Special Educational Needs) Regulations 1994;*

- *Education (Special Educational Needs) (Information) Regulations 1994.*

Specific information on policy and practice is now required by law but it is important to remember that what schools decide to do will vary according to their size, organisation, extent of need and resourcing levels. Each policy not only needs to meet the legal information requirements but also to reflect the ***unique working practice*** of the school itself.

In addition schools need to consider the package of six Circulars on 'Pupils with Problems'. (DFE 1994, *Circulars 8/94 - 13/94.*) The *Code of Practice* applies equally to children whose learning is affected by emotional and behavioural difficulties. However, although there are sometimes significant similarities in strategies and approaches to be used in both these areas of need, there are sufficient differences to make it important to produce ***two distinct policies***. Each of these, whilst being consistent with each other, should have a sharp focus on that particular aspect of the school's work. It should be remembered, too, that when schools are inspected by OFSTED, (Office for Standards in Education), 'Behaviour and Discipline' and 'Special Educational Needs' will be considered as two distinct aspects and, whilst consistency of approach and effectiveness of communication systems between these two aspects are of importance, nonetheless there are separate issues to consider in each case. (*OFSTED Handbook for the Inspection of Schools,* revised May, 1994.)

Not so long ago, schools were being advised to keep policies short and to the point. The policy outlined on one side of A4 was regarded as having particular merit. However, the current requirement to produce specific information in special needs policies does mean that ***a lengthier document is required***. Schools are advised to work through each of the headings and make sure they have met all the information requirements and outlined how these are translated into practice in their school. Section 6 (Additional Guidelines) does not constitute a legal requirement but provides advice about ways of extending the policy into working practice.

The areas considered in this document are:
- the reasons for policy;

- staff and governor involvement in policy development;

- the timescale;

- information required to be published in policies;

- additional guidelines;

- school success criteria;

- the monitoring and reporting arrangements;

- producing a policy for special educational needs.

2 - Reasons for Formulating a Policy

The issues to be considered by schools when drawing up and reporting annually to parents on their SEN policies are now legally defined by the legislation.

OFSTED Inspectors - will be required to comment on the effectiveness of SEN policies and practices for identifying, assessing and making provision for children's special educational needs. *'Special Educational Needs'* is an important aspect within the Framework for Inspection. Every subject inspector, as well as the specialist SEN inspector, is required to consider how effectively special educational needs are met within the primary school. Being able to provide a clear up-to-date policy in advance of the inspection will obviously set the process off to a good start.

Public accountability - is also emphasised in the legislation. Parents of children with special needs are entitled to receive information on the school's SEN policy and on the support available within the school and the LEA. Parents have a right to be informed about their role in assessment and decision making. Information should be given out on services such as those provided by the local authority for children 'in need' and on local and national voluntary organisations which might provide information, advice or counselling. It follows that partnership with parents needs to be embedded into every aspect of policy and that the policy should be written in such a way that it is readily understandable by parents. It is advisable to ensure that parents have access to the DFE booklet *Special Educational Needs: a Guide for Parents,* (1994) which outlines parental rights.

Governors - also have important duties and responsibilities in relation to children with special needs. As well as helping to devise policy, governors must report annually to parents on the implementation of policy according to set criteria. More specific information on their overall responsibilities is outlined in *Figure 1* and their role in monitoring and reporting on policy in Section 7.

However, most crucially of all, discussion of policy issues *improves the understanding and awareness* of all staff. The effective implementation of policy should improve *the quality of teaching and learning* for all pupils with special educational needs. That is why the information requirements of the *Code of Practice* and the additional *Regulations* should be supplemented by practical **guidelines** which will support the development of good practice in the classroom.

3 - A Whole School Approach to Policy Development

The *Code* makes it clear that provision for pupils with special educational needs is a matter for the school as a whole. The governing body, the school's headteacher, SEN co-ordinator (or team) and all members of staff have important duties and responsibilities in terms of policy development. It is important that these are clearly defined and not regarded as solely the responsibility of the Special Educational Needs Co-ordinator (SENCo). Further guidance about producing the policy is provided in Section 8.

The school's governing body
The *Code of Practice* envisages a close partnership between the school and the governing body and gives a clear message that SEN policy development is an important issue to consider at a senior level and that resourcing needs to be at a realistic level to implement the policy.

'The governing body should, in co-operation with the headteacher, determine the school's general policy and approach to provision for children with special educational needs, establish the appropriate staffing and funding arrangements and maintain a general oversight of the school's work'.) (*Code of Practice 2.7.*)

Schools will need to consider how they are going to ensure that this liaison takes place. The *Code* suggests that the governing body may appoint a committee to take a particular interest in monitoring the school's work.

Alternatively, a named governor should be identified who can work closely with the school's senior management team on the task of devising policy and overseeing its implementation.

Headteachers
Headteachers, too, have key responsibilities. They must determine the school's general policy and approach to provision, establish the appropriate staffing and funding arrangements and maintain general oversight of the school's work.

SENCO and all staff
Paragraph 2.7 of the *Code* also reminds us that, as well as headteacher and governing body involvement in policy development, the SENCo and all teaching and non-teaching staff should be involved.

Schools will, therefore, need to consider how all members of staff are involved in the discussion of policy issues. It is advisable to identify staff training times when these matters can be addressed.

The *Code* also reminds us at 2.7 that the SENCo (or team) working closely with fellow teachers has responsibility for the day-to-day operation of the school's policy.

Parents
Whilst parents do not legally have a role in devising policy, they are entitled to receive information about the policy and its implementation.

In view of the considerable emphasis that the *Code* places on partnership with parents at every stage (*Code of Practice 2.33*) schools may wish to arrange a meeting for parents to ensure that parents understand the policy and to comment upon it if they wish.

Summary of duties and responsibilities
Figure 1 on Page 8 shows a summary of the main duties and responsibilities of those involved in the implementation of the *Code of Practice*.

Policy Development for Special Educational Needs: A Primary School Approach

Figure 1 - Working Together to Implement the Code of Practice

	SEN POLICY ISSUES	OTHER DUTIES AND RESPONSIBILITIES
LEA	• determines the overall policy for all aspects of a quality service for children with special needs.	• formula for resourcing special needs; • management of assessment and statementing procedures; • named officers to deal with processes; • consistency of proformas used; • governor training needs; • maintains overview of policy and practice.
GOVERNORS	• determine school policy with headteacher including staffing and funding arrangements; • report annually to parents on systems for identification, assessment, provision, monitoring and record keeping, and use of outside Support Services; • may consult the LEA, the FAS and neighbouring schools about policy.	• must have regard for the *Code of Practice*; • do their best to secure appropriate provision is made; • ensure staff know about children's special needs and the importance of identifying and providing for them; • may appoint SEN Sub-Committee; • may appoint a named governor.
HEAD	• determines school policy with governors including staffing and funding arrangements; • ensures full staff participation in policy development; • ensures policy is delivered and monitored; • may consult the LEA, the FAS and neighbouring schools about policy.	• establishes quality provision which reflects policy; • ensures confidentiality of information, as appropriate; • may modify or disapply the National Curriculum; • continued responsibility during statutory assessment/statementing procedures; • keeps governing body informed on SEN issues; • may be named person for SEN; • ensures adequate INSET arrangements for all staff.

© Kathleen Luton, 1995
NASEN Enterprises Ltd.

	SEN POLICY ISSUES	OTHER DUTIES AND RESPONSIBILITIES
SENCO	<ul><li>assists in devising and writing policy;</li><li>oversees day-to-day operation of the policy;</li><li>ensures effective communication between staff and policy issues.</li></ul>	<ul><li>maintains school's SEN register;</li><li>provides support and advice at Stage 1;</li><li>takes a lead role at Stages 2 and 3 (onwards);</li><li>oversees all records and ensures correct documentation available for statutory assessment;</li><li>liaises with parents and outside agencies;</li><li>contributes to in-service training.</li></ul>
ALL TEACHING STAFF	<ul><li>assist in devising policy;</li><li>ensure that subject policies and schemes of work refer to SEN policy and are consistent with it.</li></ul>	<ul><li>deliver quality practice for children with special needs;</li><li>collect accurate information when there are concerns at Stage 1;</li><li>assist with implementation of IEPs at Stages 2 and 3 (onwards);</li><li>liaise with SENCo on children with special needs.</li></ul>
NON TEACHING STAFF	<ul><li>make a contribution to policy development.</li></ul>	<ul><li>support teachers in delivering quality practice for children with special needs.</li></ul>
PARENTS	<ul><li>receive copy of policy which fulfils the information requirements of the *Education (Special Educational Needs) (Information) Regulations (1994)*;</li><li>informed of all measures the school proposes to take in terms of assessment, provision and review.</li></ul>	<ul><li>work in partnership with school and other professionals involved;</li><li>provide information which will help the school in understanding the child's needs;</li><li>give help at home;</li><li>support the implementation of the individual education plan;</li><li>involved in reviews of progress.</li></ul>
WORKING TOGETHER TO IMPLEMENT THE CODE OF PRACTICE		

© Kathleen Luton, 1995
NASEN Enterprises Ltd.

4 - The Timescale

Schools must have regard to the *Code of Practice* as from September 1994.

OFSTED inspectors will expect schools to have regard to the *Code* from this date. In practice, this means that schools should be able to provide an action plan showing how they are meeting the requirements of the *Code of Practice*. There is flexibility within the *Code*, however, and there will be differing rates of progress in relation to the level of challenge faced by individual schools.

Information on policies ***must be produced by 1 August 1995***. Governors must report on the implementation and success of the policy in their first annual report after this date.

Schools will be required to summarise their policies in their prospectuses from August 1995.

Schools therefore need to identify the critical tasks which need to be undertaken during the academic year previously reviewed in order to ensure their policies meet legal requirements and are regularly monitored.

It is suggested that, as part of the school development planning process, every school should consider targets for special educational needs and implement and review these in the light of the *Code of Practice*.

5 - The Contents of Policy

This booklet will now take each of the content requirements of the *Code* and outline the issues which policies must address.

After each section there are some check points for schools to consider when writing the policy content. They do ***not*** serve as an exhaustive list but should help to illustrate some of the issues which need to be considered.

It is for schools themselves to decide the level of detail they wish to include under each heading. However, the ***written style*** needs to be accessible to parents and outside agencies as well as teachers and governors.

It is important to note that the following are ***minimum requirements*** for a policy. There are many additional aspects of delivery which each school needs to work out to meet its own needs most effectively.

5.1 - Summary Statement

Every policy needs a starting point. The starting point in this case is to make sure the school has discussed the main ***principles*** of the Code and how it will convert these into working reality.

The main principles are as follows:
- There is a continuum of special educational needs which should be matched by a continuum of provision in schools.

- All children with special educational needs must have their needs addressed.

- Children with special educational needs should have the greatest possible access to a broad and balanced education including the National Curriculum.

- Most children with special educational needs, including those with statements should be educated in mainstream schools alongside their peers.

- Pre-school children with special educational needs may require the intervention of the LEA and the Health Services.

- The involvement of parents is vital. A partnership throughout assessment, delivery and review is a key element of the *Code*.

- Provision should match the nature of the child's special educational needs.

- Careful objective recording is required throughout.

- Wherever possible, the child's views must be ascertained, recorded and taken into account when planning provision.

Having considered these principles, the policy could begin with a short ***summary statement*** about the beliefs which all staff and governors share in relation to pupils with special needs.

Check points

- Has the school arrived at a **consensus view** about policy and provision for children with special needs?

- Has the school set up a **process of consultation** for considering the summary statement and objectives?

- Is the summary statement **readily understandable** by parents, as well as school and governors?

- Are the principles of **collaboration, equality of access** and the **development of potential** contained within the statement?

5.2 - Objectives

Objectives describe in more detail the main goals that the school wishes to achieve. Schools need to set aside time to clarify and update these.

They should be discussed by all staff, both teaching and non-teaching, and by governors. They should obviously be consistent with the summary statement and the key principles of the *Code*. Subject policies should also contain the subject specific objectives for children with special educational needs and these should be consistent with the special needs policy.

> **Check points**
>
> Do the objectives refer to:
>
> - a clear framework for the implementation of the *Code of Practice?*
>
> - the duties and responsibilities of members of staff at each stage?
>
> - access for pupils to a broad and balanced curriculum appropriate to the individual's special educational needs?
>
> - the statutory rights of parents?
>
> - procedures undertaken by school and outside agencies?
>
> - accurate assessment, differentiated provision and the requirements for record keeping?
>
> - the use made of information technology?

5.3 - The Management of Special Educational Needs

Paragraph 2.14 of the *Code* makes it clear that the special needs co-ordinator plays a pivotal role in co-ordinating and delivering effective education for children with special educational needs. Schools should consider carefully each aspect of the job description listed below and then describe in their policy the arrangements they have made for the management and delivery of provision. The SENCo's job description should be reviewed annually in the light of school needs and the demands of the *Code of Practice.*

> 'In all mainstream schools a designated teacher should be responsible for:
>
> - the day-to-day operation of the school's SEN policy;
>
> - liaising with and advising fellow teachers;
>
> - co-ordinating provision for children with special needs;
>
> - maintaining the school's SEN register and overseeing the records on all pupils with special educational needs;
>
> - liaising with parents of children with special educational needs;
>
> - contributing to the in-service training of staff;
>
> - liaising with external agencies including the educational psychology service and other support agencies, medical and social services and voluntary bodies'.

Figure 2 - The School's SEN Co-ordinator (taken from The Code of Practice, 1994 Paragraph 2.14).

This does not constitute an exhaustive list. There are additional responsibilities assigned to the SENCo at various stages of the *Code*. There are requirements to assess pupils' needs, gather new information if necessary and ensuring individual education plans are drawn up and reviewed with parents from Stage 2 onwards *(Code of Practice 2.93.)*

However, it would certainly be contrary to the development of *a whole school approach to special educational needs* if a review of the role of the Special Educational Needs Co-ordinator did not go alongside a review of the responsibilities of *all* members of staff. Clearly, every teacher, as well as the SENCo, has a responsibility for 'the day-to-day operation of the school's SEN policy'. *All* teachers need to know about the requirements of the *Code* and their responsibility for developing quality practice at each stage. Whilst the SENCo ensures that the individual education plan is drawn up, it is envisaged that the class teacher and curriculum specialists would have a contribution to make in terms of setting appropriate goals, delivery and review. In most schools Individual Education Plans (IEPs) will, in the main, be delivered within normal classroom settings and therefore it is entirely appropriate that all staff understand the process and contribute to it.

There are key decisions for each school to make in terms of deciding the level of responsibility to be held by the Special Needs Co-ordinator, the extent of non contact time needed for administrative duties and whether the Co-ordinator can be expected to carry out other school responsibilities in addition to their responsibilities for special educational needs. The enormous variety of schools and the challenges faced by them makes it difficult to be unduly prescriptive about the ideal working arrangements for the SENCo. It is important however, that they are given the *time* and *status* within the school to carry out their duties effectively.

Check points

- Have the responsibilities of class/subject teachers for the day-to-day teaching of SEN pupils been clearly defined?

- Are the administrative and teaching duties of the SENCo clearly and realistically described?

- Are the management responsibilities of staff with a major pastoral role described?

- Do the arrangements make clear how consultation and information sharing take place?

- Has the overall management role of the headteacher and senior management team been clearly outlined?

5.4 - Admission Arrangements

Schools and LEAs must consider their policies on pupils with SEN but without a statement in the context of their overall admission arrangements.

Circular 6/93, Admissions to Maintained Schools gives guidance on suitable admission arrangements. Whilst LEAs and schools can make any reasonable and objective admission arrangements in the event of over-subscription, those arrangements cannot be used to refuse admission to a child - or give lower priority than other applicants - simply because the school considers that it cannot cater for his or her special educational needs.

Admission arrangements can *give priority* to children with special educational needs. Your school's policy should state whether the admission arrangements do give such priority and, if so, what criteria are used. It should also state the kind of information about the child the school would need to consider in deciding whether a child's SEN would meet the criteria.

Where the school caters for a particular specialism the SEN policy should also specify whether the school or LEA gives priority in admitting children who could make use of such facilities. (See 5.5).

Check points

- Are the admission arrangements for non-statemented pupils with special needs clearly stated in the SEN policy?

- Are these consistent with LEA policy and non-discriminatory?

- Where the school's admissions policy does give priority to children with special educational needs is this clearly stated in the school prospectus?

5.5 - SEN Specialisms and Special Units
The policy must describe:
- any particular SEN, of which the school has experience, and in which it has some expertise;

- any special unit within the school, for example, speech and language, visual, hearing;

- the expertise of staff;

- any special equipment available;

- the arrangements for the support of children in units;

- their integration with the work of the school as a whole.

Check points

- Is there a consistent approach to policy development shared by Unit and mainstream?

- Where two distinct policies are written are these appropriately cross-referenced?

- Are areas of responsibility and channels of communication between Unit and mainstream clearly described?

- Are criteria for integration clear, realistic and workable?

- Are teaching arrangements in the Unit described?

- Are the arrangements for support in mainstream described?

- Are the systems for monitoring and evaluating the work of the Unit made clear?

5.6 - Access for disabled pupils and adults

Schools which have access for pupils and adults with disabilities should describe their particular arrangements within their special needs policies. These may include wheelchair access, ramps and handrails.

Check points

- Has the school considered the extent of its accessibility for disabled pupils and adults?

- Where the school has partial accessibility has this been made clear in the policy?

- Are any specialist facilities described?

- Is the description positively phrased even in those cases where access is difficult?

5.7 - The Allocation of Resources

All schools which are locally managed receive some funding for additional special educational needs. The policy must describe the ***principles*** governing the school's allocation of resources to, and between, pupils with special educational needs. Schools should be able to demonstrate ways in which pupils with SENs have benefited; for example through the provision of incentive allowances, the purchase of additional staffing, or books, materials and equipment.

Where schools have delegated resources to meet the needs of pupils with statements, the school's policy should explain how the governing body has allocated funds to ensure that the provision specified in statements is made, in fulfilment of governors' responsibilities.

Although it is at the discretion of governing bodies as to how money is allocated, the school's policy should explain how the governing body ensure that funds are used to help them fulfil their duties under the *Education Act 1993*. (Section 161 (1) (a)).

Governing bodies may spend more than the LEA notional allocation.

When schools are inspected by OFSTED they will be required to account for how the additional funding has been spent to support children with special needs.

Check points

- Has the governing body, together with the headteacher, articulated the principles upon which it allocates resources to pupils with special needs?

- Are these principles consistent with the *Code of Practice*?

- Are these systems in place to ensure that resources for SEN pupils are efficiently used in practice? What are the monitoring arrangements?

- Does the policy state how statemented pupils benefit from funds allocated to them?

5.8 - Identification and Assessment: Record Keeping and Review

Policies should describe the arrangements for keeping and updating the *special needs register* and the confidential nature of this.

The Code gives very little guidance about the purpose of keeping a register - but reminds SENCos that it is their responsibility to keep one for the school. *(Code of Practice 2.14.)*

Keeping a register can fulfil a number of important functions for the school:

- It shows at a glance all the children who are receiving special educational needs support within the school.

- It provides the statistical information on the numbers of children at each of the stages of the *Code*.

- It signals that, for each of these children, there is some additional documentation available showing what support is being given.

- It should provide accurate information which can guide school development planning for special educational needs and provide a prompt for targeting INSET initiatives.

- It could be used to build up information and provide useful comparative data against which schools could measure the success of their performance.

Examples:

- Does the register show an increase/decrease of numbers of children with special educational needs year on year?

- How many pupils are effectively helped and move off the register?

- Are there any implications in terms of the ethnic or gender breakdown of pupils on the register?

It can be seen, therefore, that the compilation of a register is an important process in terms of establishing and maintaining accurate identification and assessment procedures. However, parents and children have a right to confidentiality and the whole school register should not be widely photocopied. Clearly, staff will know the information about the children they teach on a class basis, but it is suggested that the whole-school register should be centrally located with the SENCo and the headteacher. Where there is a named governor for special educational needs, s/he will need to know the basic statistical information but does not need to know actual children's names. The register should also be available to external monitoring agencies such as OFSTED (Office for Standards in Education) and to support services.

The policy will need, also, to outline its system for identifying special needs including the use of screening or assessment tools. These will need to be considered alongside National Curriculum Assessments.

Assessment tests should, as far as possible, be culturally fair and useful for a range of ethnic groups.

Schools will also need to outline their systems for the transfer of information on pupils with SEN between phases and between schools.

Schools will need to outline their procedures for dealing with the school-based stages of assessment, record keeping and review. They will also need to ensure that parents are fully informed about procedures used at every stage.

It is important to ensure that assessment and record keeping procedures remain manageable and fulfil their essential purpose of supporting children's progress.

Systems for involving parents, pupils and outside agencies should also be outlined within the policy.

Check points

- Has a clear statement been made about the nature and purpose of the special needs register?

- Are there agreed criteria for placing children in the register?

- Have assessment and record keeping arrangements at each stage been discussed by staff and written into the policy?

- Has the role of the SENCo in assessment and record keeping been described?

- Are the review arrangements clearly described?

- Are the arrangements for the transfer of information between phases and between schools clear?

- Does this system make clear how parents, pupils and outside agencies are involved?

5.9 - Integration Arrangements

This section reinforces Section 161 (4) of the *Education Act 1993* which states that governing bodies must ensure that pupils with special needs receive equality of entitlement and are integrated into all the activities of the school as far as it is practical and compatible with SEN pupils receiving the necessary educational provision, the efficient education of other children and the efficient use of resources.

The examples given in *Circular 6.94*, Paragraphs 45 - 47, refer to the social integration of children who are predominantly in a unit at the school and the physical accessibility of any rooms used by such pupils.

Schools should ensure that this principle is included within their statements of objectives, (Section 5.2), and embedded in all other sections of the policy.

Check points

- Is it clear from the policy that pupils with special educational needs receive equality of entitlement to all activities?

- Where there is a Unit, has policy and practice been reviewed to ensure equality of entitlement to all activities?

5.10 - Parental Involvement

The school's policy must outline arrangements for working with parents under three main headings: *Information, Partnership* and *Access*. The detail under these headings is as follows:

Information

- on the school's SEN policy;

- on the support available for children with special educational needs within the school and LEA;

- on parents' involvement in assessment and decision-making, emphasising the importance of their contribution;

- on services such as those provided by the local authority for children 'in need';

- on local and national voluntary organisations which might provide information, advice or counselling.

Partnership

- arrangements for recording and acting upon parental concerns;

- procedures for involving parents when a concern is first expressed within the school;

- arrangements for incorporating parents' views in assessment and subsequent reviews.

Access for Parents

- information in a range of community languages;

- information on tape for parents who may have literacy or communication difficulties;

- a parents' room or other arrangements in the school to help parents feel confident and comfortable.

Figure 3 - taken from The Code of Practice, 1994, Paragraph 2.33.

As well as a specific section on partnership with parents, all other sections of the policy should refer, as appropriate, to parental involvement.

Check points

- Has the school reviewed its general policy about contact with parents and the stages at which senior management should become involved/take the lead?

- Are the arrangements for parental contact made clear in the SEN policy and the school prospectus?

- Are the lists of support services and local and national voluntary organisations readily available to them?

5.11 - LEA Support Services

The policy should state the school's arrangements for securing access to external support services. These may include: Support Services for Pupils with Specific Learning Difficulties; Educational Psychologists; Education Welfare Services; Social Services, and Behaviour Support Services. Parents should know about the support which is available to them.

Check points

- Does the policy include an up-to-date list of LEA support services and their roles?

- Have parents been made aware of the support which is available?

5.12 - Links with Health, Social Services and Voluntary Organisations

The policy should explain the school's arrangements for how they work in partnership and exchange information with other services. Parents are entitled to receive information on these services, together with appropriate information on local and national voluntary organisations which might provide information, advice or counselling.

The DFE's *Special Educational Needs - Guide for Parents* (1994) provides a list of useful addresses at the back but it would be advisable to add to them those which have been found useful on a local basis.

Check points

- Does the policy explain how links are made with these services and the roles they fulfil?

- Does the policy include a list of national and local voluntary organisations?

5.13 - Links with other Mainstream and Special Schools

The policy should set out any arrangement, whereby the school draws upon expertise in other mainstream schools, special schools or resource centres. Any arrangements for integrating special school pupils into mainstream should be described and any arrangements whereby mainstream pupils benefit from special school settings.

Check points

- Does the policy describe how links with other mainstream and special schools have been forged?

- Does it describe the extent of any projects which have been developed and how these are monitored and evaluated?

5.14 - Experience, Qualifications and In-Service Training

The policy must state any relevant qualifications and experience of staff with particular responsibility for pupils with special educational needs. It must set out the school's in-service training policy for SEN including any joint arrangements with other schools.

> **Check points**
>
> - Has the school considered the principles upon which it has delegated funding for SEN training?
>
> - What are the details of that funding?
>
> - Has the school ensured adequate in-service training for SEN and included its arrangements within the policy?
>
> - Does the policy describe any shared arrangements with other schools or consortia?

5.15 - Success Criteria for School Policies

Having devised the policy and given consideration to practical guidelines which need to be developed, each school needs to consider what success criteria it will adopt.

In developing such criteria it is advisable to bear in mind that there is also a requirement on the governing body to comment on the success of the school's policy for pupils with special educational needs in their annual report to parents.

> In commenting on the success of the policy, the report should demonstrate the effectiveness of the school's systems for:
>
> - identification;
>
> - assessment;
>
> - provision;
>
> - monitoring and record keeping;
>
> - use of outside support services and agencies.

Figure 4 - Commenting on the success of the policy in the governors' annual report (taken from The Code of Practice, 1994, Paragraph 2.12).

As with any other school based initiative, it is worth remembering that the targets should be:

        Specific

        Measurable

        Attainable

        Relevant

        Time constrained

It is important that the SENCo works alongside **all** staff in developing success criteria for the policy. Such criteria should be personalised to the school's current developmental state in relation to special educational needs and be set in the context of the level of challenge faced and available resources.

Some examples of success criteria which schools might like to consider are listed below. It is not suggested that the entire list is pertinent to all schools as this will depend upon that level of good practice which has already developed:

- The school has clear procedures for identifying pupils with special educational needs, using National Curriculum Assessments and additional diagnostic SEN Assessments and tests.

- There is a system in place for measuring the progress of pupils with special educational needs through the Action Plans for pupils at Stage 1 and the Individual Education Plans for pupils at Stage 2 onwards.

- The school has successfully moved (X) per cent of pupils who were at Stage 3 to Stage 2, (X) per cent from Stage 2 to Stage 1 and (X) per cent from Stage 1 off the Register of Special Educational Need.

- A resource base of materials for pupils with special educational needs has been developed by curriculum postholders together with the SENCo.

- A record keeping system for the *Code of Practice* has been developed, teachers understand their role at each stage and time has been identified for class teachers to liaise with the SENCo.

- Parents are aware of the contents of the school policy and have been informed their rights and responsibilities.

- All teaching and non teaching staff have received a programme of INSET about the *Code of Practice*.

Check points

- Have all teaching and non-teaching staff been involved in developing policy? Do they understand it? Is it realistic and workable?

- Are parents happy with the information available to them, the quality of educational provision and the system of communication with the school?

- Have the requirements of the Education (Special Educational Needs) (Information) Regulations been met in the policy?

- Is the policy supported by the development of practical guidelines which make a real difference to classroom practice and raising standards of achievement?

- Are subject policies cross-referenced to the special needs policy?

- Does the policy documentation satisfy external monitoring agencies such as the LEA and OFSTED?

5.16 - Dealing with Parents' Complaints

Every school needs a system for considering parental complaints about SEN provision within the school. This should be consistent with the school's general complaints procedure and should be outlined in the school's SEN policy and the prospectus.

Parents should be given the name of the person to whom they can complain if discussion with the class teacher and SENCo fails to resolve the problem. This should normally be the headteacher.

Check points

- Are parents informed about who they should contact if they have any queries or complaints about provision for pupils with special needs?

- Has the school considered its overall policy about counselling and supporting parents?

---

6 - Additional Guidelines

This section does not constitute a legal requirement but gives examples of ways in which policy can be extended into working practice.

In addition to all the above information requirements the *Code* also requires school policies to describe:

'arrangements for providing access to the curriculum for pupils with SEN to a balanced and broadly based curriculum, including the National Curriculum'.

(Code of Practice 2.10, Point 2.)

It is important that policies actually **make a difference** in the classroom and improve the quality of teaching and learning which takes place. The information requirements are extensive but the provision of detailed information is not sufficient in terms of improving classroom practice. The *Code* says little about *how* issues are to be addressed in the classroom.

As well as addressing issues of information, it is important for schools to consider the development of ***practical guidelines*** which will be useful to every practitioner. Guidelines addressing the 'How?' issues need to be developed by every school. Most schools are already in the process of doing this and can provide documentation on a range of topics, for example: Classroom organisation; the teaching of reading, spelling and handwriting; differentiation.

In the remainder of this section can be found some examples of practical guidelines which schools should consider developing. These could appear as separate ***appendices*** to the main policy so that each can be distributed, as appropriate, to teaching and non-teaching staff, parents and governors.

6.1 - Classroom Support

A range of support for pupils with special educational needs may be available within the school and from outside support services. This may include:

- ***The SENCo*** acting as support teacher in implementing IEPs at Stage 2 onwards.

- *Curriculum Co-ordinators* who have a role in assisting with the development of good practice for pupils with SEN in the context of their subject.

- *External Specialist Services* such as the support services for pupils with specific learning difficulties, who will be assisting in devising and delivering IEPs at Stage 3 onwards.

- *Classroom Assistants* who may be specifically designated to teach statemented pupils and/or other pupils with special educational needs.

- *Parents* who, under the direction of the teacher, may be helping to make resources, hearing children read or helping with writing activities.

Schools need to have clear guidelines about how the range of expertise available should be utilised within the school.

Good support teaching requires effective planning so that methods of working together, aims, required outcomes and monitoring and evaluation are built into the system. (See Appendix A.)

6.2 - Planning for Individual Needs

Stage 1 of the *Code of Practice* requires teachers to keep a record of the ***differentiated*** teaching which has taken place for pupils with special educational needs. Individual Education Plans (IEPs) form a major part of the teaching delivery from Stage 2 onwards. Many LEAs have provided schools with pro-formas for these plans and additional guidance about how to use them. Any additional guidelines produced by the school should refer to how these will operate in the particular school setting. The guidelines should refer to the scope of the IEP, whether they will be operated on an in-class or a withdrawal basis, or a combination of these methods. They should refer to how they are to be used alongside other planning documentation used by the class/subject teacher, the monitoring arrangements and pupil and parental involvement.

(Examples of Stage 1 Action Plans and Stage 2 and 3 IEPs are provided at Appendix B.)

Every subject policy should also refer to the place of Individual Education Plans within the teaching of that subject. Individual Education Plans form one method by which the curriculum is differentiated for particular pupils and will need to be incorporated in to every teacher's working practice.

The *Code* also draws attention to the use of information technology as a means of providing individualised support. Schools need to consider incorporating Information Technology based targets into IEPs where these will aid the child's progress.

6.3 - Differentiation

The variety of methods by which schools differentiate the curriculum need to be clearly outlined within additional guidelines. OFSTED inspectors frequently refer to this issue when describing the quality of teaching and learning. The main forms of differentiation for which schools need to develop additional guidance are described below. (For more detailed guidance see *Differentiation: Ways Forward* edited by Margaret Peter, published by NASEN Enterprises):

- by organisational styles used;

- by text/resources used;

- by task;

- by support;

- by outcome.

(See Appendix C)

6.4 - Paired/Shared Reading

The roles of staff, goals, nature of the programme, specific activities and monitoring and evaluation need to be considered where this initiative takes place. The role of parents in supporting children with special educational needs is strongly emphasised in the *Code of Practice*. It would be helpful to review any information currently sent out to parents about supporting reading to ensure that it makes reference to the *Code of Practice*.

(See Appendix D)

7 - The Monitoring and Reporting Arrangements

(See the diagram in Section 3 for main duties and responsibilities)

The governing body may wish to appoint a committee to take a particular interest in and closely monitor the school's work on behalf of children with special needs.

The headteacher is responsible for day-to-day management of all aspects of the school's work including special educational needs and will need to keep the governing body fully informed. It is advisable to include the updating of special needs policy and provision within the School Development Plan.

The policy must be published by 1st August 1995. The first annual report to parents after the publication of the policy must comment on the implementation of the policy.

The governing body must include information on:

- the success of the SEN policy;

- significant changes in the policy;

- any consultation with the LEA, the Funding Authority and other schools;

- how resources have been allocated to and amongst children with special educational needs over the year.

(Education (Special Educational Needs) (Information) Regulations, Regulation 5 and Schedule 4.)

In commenting on the success of the policy, the report should demonstrate the school's effectiveness on identification, assessment, provision, monitoring and record keeping and use of outside support services. (Section 5.15.)

Summaries of the SEN policy must appear in the school prospectus in the Autumn of 1995.

It should be remembered that OFSTED inspections will consider the effectiveness of school's policies and practices for identifying, assessing and making provision for pupils' special educational needs.

8 - Producing a Policy for Special Educational Needs

This booklet has considered all the content areas which need to be considered in order to update policies. Clearly, schools will be at various stages in the process and the Special Needs Policy Review Guide (Appendix E) can help to generate discussion amongst all staff about the school's current achievements and what remains to be done. The Review Guide headings include all the information requirements of the *Code of Practice* and the *Education (Special Educational Needs) Regulations,* 1994. Provided schools address these headings - and, of course, some of the headings may be placed in a different order - the policy will meet statutory requirements.

The following is a suggested sequence of action which schools may find helpful:

1. SENCo to receive INSET about the *Code of Practice.*

2. SENCo (supported by senior management team) to provide INSET to colleagues about the basic principles of the *Code of Practice,* the staged approach and implications for classroom practice.

3. SENCo to circulate the **Special Needs Policy Review Guide** for each member of staff to complete.

4. SENCo (supported by a member of the senior management team) to collate responses.

5. Feedback to be given to staff about all the *positive aspects* which have been marked with a YES. Those with a NO can then be considered by the whole staff. It may be, that after shared discussion, some of the NOs can actually be answered affirmatively using the collective wisdom of the staff. Some of the DON'T KNOWs may also be easily resolved in this way. Statements which remain as definite NOs will provide the whole school with priority areas for development. Staff should be encouraged to rank the priority areas according to the school's needs.

6. Action plan to be drawn up and implemented (See Appendix F).

7. A date for review of the policy should be agreed.

Policy Development for Special Educational Needs: A Primary School Approach
Appendix A - Allsorts JI School Guidelines for Classroom Support

(These areas are our focus for 1995 - 1996. This is not an exhaustive list.)

	ROLE	ACTION	SUCCESS CRITERIA
SENCo	• advice on developing teaching strategies for less able pupils; • advice on adapting teaching materials; • advice on classroom organisation; • support in delivering IEPs at Stage 2 onwards.	• time identified by the school for giving support; • joint planning with class teachers; • adapted worksheets/materials; • ongoing assessment of SEN pupils; • goals of IEPs delivered alongside class teacher.	• running record of SENCo support to be kept; • IEPs implemented and checked for progress made; • range of adapted worksheets in resource base.
CURRICULUM CO-ORDINATORS	• support to colleagues in developing differentiated practice in the context of their subject specialism.	• one session to be provided for each class teacher per term; • preparation of list of SEN resources appropriate for KS1 and KS2 in subject specialism; • provide at least one new approach for the class teacher to use with underachieving pupils.	• curriculum co-ordinators to keep running record of support given; • evaluation by class teachers of the new approach/strategies tried with under achieving pupils.
EXTERNAL SUPPORT SERVICES Behaviour Support Psychological Service Pupil and School Support Service	• to advise on behaviour problems and to help devise, implement and review IEPs; • to advise on assessment and statementing procedures and to help in devising, implementing and reviewing IEPs; • to advise on a range of learning difficulties and to help devise, implement and review IEPs.	• Behaviour Support Service to provide INSET session about methods of classroom support for pupils with behavioural problems; • EP to carry out additional class based observation of pupils being considered for Stage 4; • P & SSS and EP to help SENCo devise IEPs at Stage 3.	• agreed shared targets between school and services; • Stage 3 IEPs more specific to individual needs; • advice at reviews has provided a clear way forward.
CLASSROOM ASSISTANTS	• to work under the direction of the teacher, supporting designated groups/individuals with SEN.	• hear children read as required by teachers; • assist with writing activities - selected pupils; • make work cards and games to supplement reading scheme, (SENCo to advise).	• pupils who require extra reading support are clearly identified and classroom assistants know how to complete the reading records; • additional resources made for SEN pupils.
PARENTS	• to work under the direction of the teacher supporting designated groups/individuals with SEN.	• assist with reading related activities; • assist with the making of materials and resources for SEN pupils.	• extra reading support given and recorded; • additional resources made for SEN pupils; • increased parental involvement.

© Kathleen Luton, 1995
NASEN Enterprises Ltd.

Policy Development for Special Educational Needs: A Primary School Approach

Appendix B1

STAGE 1 ACTION PLAN

Pupil's name: PAUL   D.O.B.:

School: ALLSORTS J + I

CA: form/yr grp:

---

1. CONCERNS: STRENGTHS:

   <u>Poor progress on reading scheme.</u>   Participates in class discussions.
   Leaves book at home.   Concentrates well on drawing
   Very little independent writing.   and colouring tasks.
   Poor concentration.   Wants to improve at reading.

   Underline your priority concern.

---

2. Further information gathered about priority concern.

   See reading record and sight vocabulary checklist.
   It has proved difficult to get parental support for reading.

---

3. GOALS:

   To develop sight vocabulary using a more structured approach.

---

4. SPECIAL HELP PLANNED and method of recording:

   Continue to use Oxford Reading Tree Stage 2 - focusing on
   key words by playing word bingo.
   Use additional suggestions from teacher's book for supporting activities.
   'Sticker' rewards when he remembers to bring back book from home.

   To be given by: Date started: 20.9.94

---

5. TO BE REVIEWED ON After half term (30th October)

© Kathleen Luton, Birmingham LEA Support Services, 1995
NASEN Enterprises Ltd.

Policy Development for Special Educational Needs: A Primary School Approach

Appendix B1

PAUL	STAGE 1 ACTION PLAN (continued)

6. DATE OF REVIEW: .... 6.11.95 ....

7. REVIEW OUTCOME including parent(s)/carer(s) and pupil's views;

Paul likes the books and is gradually making progress. He has enjoyed playing word bingo with key words from the scheme.

The 'sticker' rewards for bringing back books from home worked well.

Continue with Stage 1 support.

Parents beginning to offer support at home.

Send letter to parents encouraging them to use home/school reading record.

☐ No further special help at Stage 1

☑ Continue at Stage 1

☐ Stage 2 or other outcome to be considered with SENCo

Signed: _____ Form/class teacher   Date: _____

© Kathleen Luton, Birmingham LEA Support Services, 1995
NASEN Enterprises Ltd.

Policy Development for Special Educational Needs: A Primary School Approach
Appendix B2
Individual Education Plan

SPECIAL EDUCATIONAL NEEDS STAGE 2 RECORD Number 1

School: Allsorts J. + I. 2

| Pupil's name | PAUL | DoB 8 years 4 months | CA | Form/yr group 3 |

GOALS
1. To develop reading by increasing sight vocabulary, phonic skills and comprehension ability.
2. To improve access to the whole curriculum.
3. To begin to develop independent writing.

WHAT Specific targets	HOW Methods/activities/resources	WHO/WHEN/WHERE Input by/frequency duration/location	METHOD OF RECORDING PROGRESS
① Reading. To consolidate vocabulary Stage 2 Oxford Reading Tree. Learn vocabulary from Stage 3.	Games, sentence building. Language Master. Reading the books.	Class teacher 3 x week Parents 3 x week	Vocabulary checklist. Paul's reading record.
② Identification initial letter sounds.	Scrapbook. Easy Learn 1. Games.	Senco 1 x week in class.	Pictorial record for Paul.
③ Use context clues.	Teacher prompt when hearing reading. Simple cloze based on Oxford Reading Tree.	As for target 1	Miscue analysis and reading record.
④ Access to the curriculum. Provide a variety of materials.	Shared reading with peers.	Cross-curricular work with partners during topic work.	Record of topic work. Spot checks as term progresses.
⑤ Writing. Write simple sentences independently.	Sentence making based on Oxford Reading Tree and own choice.	Senco 1 x week in class. Class teacher 2 x week in class.	Evidence of Paul's sentence writing - content and length.

Date of IEP   Proposed Review Date   Appropriate Records should be attached

© Kathleen Luton, Birmingham LEA Support Services, 1995

Policy Development for Special Educational Needs: A Primary School Approach

Appendix B3

Individual Education Plan

SPECIAL EDUCATIONAL NEEDS **STAGE 3 RECORD** Number 1

Pupil's name PAUL	DoB	CA 9 YEARS 1 MONTH	Form/yr group 4

GOALS To improve reading by increasing basic sight vocabulary; developing phonic skills and extending strategies for identifying unfamiliar words in context. To develop independent writing further and continue to improve access to the curriculum.

WHAT Specific targets	HOW Methods/activities/resources	WHO/WHEN/WHERE Input by/frequency duration/location	METHOD OF RECORDING PROGRESS
Reading ① To read vocabulary - Wellington Square Level 1 Books 1 + 2	Procedures in Wellington Square Level 1 file.	SENCO - Tues + Thurs. (group of 3 in class - 30 mins) Class teacher follow up.	Word wall and checklist.
② To consolidate C.V.C. blending (medial a/i/o). Read and write accurately words with medial e and u	As at Stage 2 with addition of plastic letters and concept keyboard program.	Pupil and Support Service (withdrawal group of 3 - 30 mins) Class teacher to follow up.	On going record of words read and spelt correctly and individual phonic record.

Date of IEP **Proposed Review Date** **Appropriate Records should be attached**

© Kathleen Luton, Birmingham LEA Support Services, 1995
NASEN Enterprises Ltd.

Policy Development for Special Educational Needs: A Primary School Approach
Appendix B3

Pupil's name PAUL   DoB   CA 9 YEARS 1 MONTH   Individual Education Plan 3 number 1 continued

WHAT Specific targets	HOW Methods/activities/ resources	WHO/WHEN/WHERE Input by/frequency duration/location	METHOD OF RECORDING PROGRESS
③ Use visual/phonic and context clues when attempting unfamiliar words.	Use appropriate prompts when hearing reading. (Class teacher will show parents how to do this). Literacy Links/Sunshine/Wellington Square.	Class teacher 3 x week (10 mins) Parents daily (10-15 mins)	Miscue analysis. After 4 weeks.
④ Writing Have confidence in writing unaided (½ page)	Encouraged to 'have a go' using known words from word wall.	Class teacher. Twice per week in English and topic lessons.	Written work checked for content, length, spelling and punctuation.
⑤ Access to the Curriculum Use at least 3 ways of recording work which don't rely on writing.	Record work by pictures/diagrams/orally - to teacher or on tape.	Class teacher. Twice per week in Science and topic lessons.	Observation of Paul's methods of reading and understanding lesson content.

© Kathleen Luton, Birmingham LEA Support Services, 1995
NASEN Enterprises Ltd.

Policy Development for Special Educational Needs: A Primary School Approach

Appendix C

Allsorts JI School
Guidelines about Differentiation

The following methods are used at Allsorts JI School. You will find that they are inter-linked. The examples are not exhaustive. INSET time will be used to focus on methods of differentiation and to consider practical ways in which staff can support one another.

1. Differentiation by organisational input

Under this heading the teacher considers all the features of organisational planning she uses to enable the most effective learning to take place.

Examples:
- class divided into ability groups - all subject areas/some subject areas;
- grouping by concentration span;
- grouping by interest;
- grouping by friendship;
- providing high/medium/low teacher intensive activities for the proposed groups;
- providing a framework of activities which have to be followed in teacher selected sequences, dependent upon the needs of the group;
- varying the delivery of teaching input eg whole class lesson followed-up by further explanation to the less able group;
- methods of deploying classroom assistants and parents to support children on IEPs.

2. Differentiation by text

Under the heading the teacher considers all the ways in which actual texts can be differentiated to suit a range of reading abilities.

Examples:
- using 'readability' tests on materials;
- using colour coding;
- simplifying chunks of text by using alternative vocabulary;
- reducing sentence length;
- reducing the amount of text to be read;
- using larger print;
- underlining the key words;
- providing more picture clues;
- using published reading schemes, reading workshops etc.

© Kathleen Luton, 1995
NASEN Enterprises Ltd.   THIS PAGE MAY BE PHOTOCOPIED

Appendix C (continued)

Allsorts JI School
Guidelines about Differentiation

3. Differentiation by task

Under this heading the teacher considers the range and suitability of tasks the children are to undertake.

Examples:
- providing individual tasks, for example, children working at own pace through Maths workbooks/cards;
- providing different tasks for different groups of children according to ability. These may be based on a single subject or a range of subjects;
- providing a run of tasks which get more difficult. The body of the task is the same for all but extension work is provided for the more able and reinforcement work for the least able;
- children carry out specific tasks described in IEPs.

4. Differentiation by support

Under this heading the teacher considers the levels of support necessary to maximise children's learning.

Examples:
- by teaching style, for example, asking the more able child the mind-stretching hypothetical question; the less able for the brief statement of fact you know they know;
- by the time/level of teaching input you give to your groups;
- by acting as the pupils' scribe;
- by providing additional clues to the answers for the less able;
- by style of marking and commenting on pupils' work, eg the very encouraging comment on a very brief piece of work which represents an excellent effect for that child.

5. Differentiation by outcome

Under this heading the teacher has a clear idea of what his/her expectations are for pupils of varying abilities. He/she also makes these clear to individual pupils.

Examples:
- by providing the same task which allows for achievement at a range of levels, for example, story writing;
- by providing open-ended tasks and setting 'markers' that you expect children of differing abilities to meet.

© Kathleen Luton, 1995
NASEN Enterprises Ltd.   THIS PAGE MAY BE PHOTOCOPIED

Policy Development for Special Educational Needs: A Primary School Approach

Appendix D

Allsorts JI School
Shared Reading

- **LIFT** is a scheme to improve children's reading.

- Many parents already read and share books with their children on a regular basis.

- At Allsorts JI School we think that reading is very important and we would like you to join in with our **LIFT** programme.

- Experience shows that children who read at home (some of the time with parents) make better progress generally than children who just read at school.

- Regular reading with your child is the best way to help them make progress and you will enjoy doing it.

- You may be asked to help with specific reading targets set out in an individual education plan for your child. It is very important that you help with these and tell us how you are getting on with them.

When should you read?

- Begin with short sessions - no more than 10 minutes at a time.

- Read with your child three times a week. You will probably find you enjoy these sessions so much that you will soon want to increase them.

Where should you read?

- Choose a quiet, comfortable part of the house where you can settle down to read in peace.

What should you read?

- We have a wide range of material chosen especially for your child - and we will help your child choose something which will interest him or her. All the reading books are carefully graded for level of reading difficulty.

© Kathleen Luton, 1995
NASEN Enterprises Ltd.   THIS PAGE MAY BE PHOTOCOPIED

What happens when your child gets stuck on a word?

Don't worry -

- Let your child have a go at guessing - the rest of the sentence might tell her or him what the word is,

    or

- wait for a few seconds; they may be trying to sort it out,

    or

- don't be afraid to actually tell them the word.

- Reading is for enjoyment, it isn't a test!

- If you are having to give your child a lot of words in each sentence, then the book is probably too difficult. So you could read it to him/her and start again with an easier book next time.

- If your child's teacher has given you any special advice to follow try this out to see if it helps.

Keeping in touch

- Your child will bring home a Reading Record card with the reading book. After each session make a comment on the amount of reading done, and the time taken, and sign the card.

- If your child is still finding reading difficult let your child's teacher know so that the reading targets can be reviewed.

Encourage your child at home and we will encourage her/him at school.

Each week your child's card will be looked at and we will use them too, to make a link with you.

Just listening to your child reading will work. It is the contact between you and your child and books that is important.

If you have any problems contact your child's class teacher who will try to help. If your child's difficulties are more severe the class teacher may refer you to our special needs co-ordinator who can provide additional advice.

© Kathleen Luton, 1995
NASEN Enterprises Ltd.   THIS PAGE MAY BE PHOTOCOPIED

Policy Development for Special Educational Needs: A Primary School Approach

Appendix E

Special Needs Policy Review Guide

Purposes: Work through the Review Guide in order to establish your current position in relation to policy issues. Then select priority areas for development in your school.

	YES	NO	DON'T KNOW
Objectives My school has a clear set of objectives for pupils with special educational needs.			
Objectives have been reviewed and are consistent with the principles of the *Code of Practice*.			
Objectives have been considered by all teaching and non-teaching staff and with the governors.			
SEN Co-ordinator We have an identified special needs co-ordinator.			
His/her job description has been updated in line with the *Code of Practice*.			
Co-ordinating Educational Provision Key tasks which require co-ordination at each of the school-based stages have been clarified.			
Staff responsibilities have been assigned within the staged model.			
Admission arrangements for non-statemented pupils Admission arrangements for pupils with special educational needs, are stated in the school's SEN policy.			
Special Units (Only for Schools with Units)			
The specialism of the Unit is described together with the expertise of staff, specialist equipment available, arrangements for support and their integration with the work of the school as a whole.			

© Kathleen Luton, 1995
NASEN Enterprises Ltd.

THIS PAGE MAY BE PHOTOCOPIED

Policy Development for Special Educational Needs: A Primary School Approach

Appendix E (continued)

Special Needs Policy Review Guide

	YES	NO	DON'T KNOW
Access for the disabled Any particular features which enable access for disabled pupils and adults are described in the policy.			
Integration arrangements The governing body has ensured that pupils with special educational needs are integrated into all the activities of the school, insofar as it is practical and compatible with the pupil receiving the necessary provision, the efficient education of other children and the efficient use of resources.			
Resources We have identified the principles governing the school's allocation of resources to pupils with special educational needs.			
The governing body has ensured that funds are used to help them fulfil their duties under the *Education Act 1993*.			
Identification and Assessment Arrangements We have an agreed system for identifying children with special educational needs, including the use of screening and assessment tools.			
We have a clear system for the transfer of information on pupils with special educational needs between phases and between schools.			
Assessment tools are culturally fair and useful for a range of ethnic groups.			
We have established a register for pupil with special educational needs.			
We have a system for involving parents and pupils in assessment arrangements.			
We have developed a staged approach to identification and assessment.			

© Kathleen Luton, 1995
NASEN Enterprises Ltd.

THIS PAGE MAY BE PHOTOCOPIED

Policy Development for Special Educational Needs: A Primary School Approach

Appendix E (continued)

Special Needs Policy Review Guide

	YES	NO	DON'T KNOW
Provision All teachers put into practice the principles of the *Code*.			
Guidelines to support effective teaching and learning for pupils with special educational needs have been devised by the school. These are regularly updated and reviewed.			
Record keeping and Review We have an agreed system for record keeping and review which is consistent with the staged approach.			
We have an agreed documentation at each stage.			
We have a system for involving parents, pupils and the support services in the review process.			
Partnership with parents We have arrangements for involving parents, recording and acting upon their concerns.			
We provide them with information on the school's policy and support available within the school and LEA.			
Support Services We have agreed procedures for involving the external support services in the context of the staged approach.			
We have agreed procedures for working in partnership with the Health Service, Social Services, Education Welfare Service and local and national voluntary organisations.			
Links with other schools We have systems for drawing upon the expertise of other mainstream schools and special schools.			
We make arrangements for integrating special school pupils into our school as appropriate.			

© Kathleen Luton, 1995
NASEN Enterprises Ltd.

THIS PAGE MAY BE PHOTOCOPIED

Policy Development for Special Educational Needs: A Primary School Approach

Appendix E (continued)

Special Needs Policy Review Guide

	YES	NO	DON'T KNOW
In-Service Training We have recorded relevant qualifications and experience of staff with particular responsibility for pupils with special educational needs.			
We have a programme for the in-service training of staff in SEN in line with the *Code of Practice*.			
Duties of Governing Bodies The governing body is aware of its duties and responsibilities under the *Code of Practice*.			
The governing body has developed a plan for implementing the requirements of the *Education Act 1993* in relation to pupils with special educational needs.			
Success Criteria We have agreed success criteria for the policy which have been shared with teaching and non-teaching staff and governors.			

Now decide which of the above you consider are the major priorities for policy development in your school.

PRIORITY AREAS FOR DEVELOPMENT

1.

2.

3.

4.

5.

6.

© Kathleen Luton, 1995
NASEN Enterprises Ltd.

THIS PAGE MAY BE PHOTOCOPIED

Policy Development for Special Educational Needs: A Primary School Approach

Appendix F

Allsorts JI School
Action Plan for Special Needs Policy Development

Goals:
1. To produce an updated special needs policy which contains all the information requirements of the *Code of Practice.*

2. To involve all teaching and non-teaching staff and governors in the development of policy.

Steps to be taken	Staff	By When?
Time in staff meeting to brainstorm special needs policy objectives.	All teaching and non-teaching staff.	Next staff meeting.
Job description of SENCo to be reviewed.	Jane (Headteacher) and Jo (SENCo).	By 31st May.
Draft register established.	Jo working with all staff on an audit of special needs.	By July.
All features which enable access for the disabled to be listed.	Jo with some advice from Pete (teacher at local PH school).	By July.
Governing body to receive INSET about their duties and responsibilities.	Jo supported by Jane.	Next full meeting of governing body.
Screening and assessment materials to be reviewed. Feedback to staff about procedures to adopt.	Mary (Assessment Coordinator) supported by Jo.	By July.
LEA documentation for the staged approach to be adopted.	All teachers. Implementation of Stage 1 Action Plans to be monitored by Key stage Co-ordinators, IEPs by Jo.	Start of Autumn Term having trialled some in Summer Term.
Parents to be informed about their rights and responsibilities.	Jane supported by Jo.	Start of Autumn Term.
All external support services to be listed. Reference directory in staff room.	Jo supported by Justin (School Secretary).	Start of Autumn Term.
Policy adopted by governing body.	Jane in discussion with governing body.	By July.

Copies: All teaching and non teaching staff
Chair of Governors.

© Kathleen Luton, 1995
NASEN Enterprises Ltd.

THIS PAGE MAY BE PHOTOCOPIED

References and Further Reading

DFE (1994) *Code of Practice on the Identification and Assessment of Special Educational Needs,* Department for Education: London.

DFE (1994) *Special Educational Needs: A Guide for Parents,* Department for Education: London.

DFE (1994) *Pupils with Problems.* Circulars 8.94 - 13.94, Department for Education: London.

Dyson, A and Gains, C (eds) (1995) The Special Educational Needs Co-ordinator. Special issue of *Support for Learning,* Vol. 10, No. 2. NASEN: Stafford.

Leadbetter, J and Leadbetter, P (1993) *Special Children - Meeting the Challenge in the Primary School,* Cassell: London.

Lunt, I, Evans, J, Norwich, B and Wedell, K (1994) *Working Together: Inter-School Collaboration for Special Needs,* David Fulton: London.

OFSTED (1994) (3rd Edition) *Handbook for the Inspection of Schools,* HMSO: London.

Peter, M (Ed) (1992) *Differentiation: Ways Forward.* NASEN: Stafford.